CARTOONING

GEORGE F. HORN
SUPERVISOR OF ART
SECONDARY SCHOOLS
BALTIMORE, MARYLAND

DAVIS PUBLICATIONS, INC. ● WORCESTER, MASSACHUSETTS

COPYRIGHT 1965
DAVIS PUBLICATIONS, INC.
WORCESTER, MASSACHUSETTS

SEVENTH PRINTING- 1979

CONTENTS

INTRODUCTION

THE CARTOON, WITH ITS CAPTIVATING SPIRIT, UNDOUBTEDLY COMMANDS MORE ATTENTION THAN ANY OTHER SINGLE ART FORM. DAILY COMIC STRIPS IN NEWSPAPERS, ILLUSTRATED JOKES IN MAGAZINES, AND THE WHOLE RANGE OF ADVERTISING MEDIA ATTEST TO THE TREMENDOUS POPULARITY OF EXCITING CREATURES OF FANTASY, BROUGHT INTO BEING BY THE PEN OF THE CARTOONIST. BUT THE CARTOON IS NOT LIMITED TO THESE AREAS ALONE. YOU PROBABLY HAVE BEEN A PART OF NUMEROUS FUNNY INCIDENTS WHICH YOU ALLOWED TO PASS ON TO OBLIVION. THE NEXT TIME SOMETHING AMUSING HAPPENS TO YOU MAKE NOTE OF IT AND THEN TRY TO EXPRESS IT WITH A CARTOON. THE PURPOSE OF THIS BOOK IS TO ASSIST YOU IN DISCOVERING YOUR OWN CARTOON STYLE. FIGURES USED TO ILLUSTRATE CERTAIN BASIC ESSENTIALS SHOULD SERVE ONLY AS A GUIDE AS YOU EXPLORE THIS WORLD OF WHIMSEY. THE EMPHASIS IS ON THE EXPRESSING OF AN IDEA AND ACHIEVING ACTION THROUGH SPARKLING EXAGGERATION, THE RIDICULOUS, AND SOMETIMES THE ABSURD. STUDY PEOPLE, ANIMALS, AND THE SCENES AROUND YOU. THE GREATER UNDERSTANDING YOU HAVE OF THESE THINGS THE GREATER YOUR SUCCESS WITH THE CARTOON. THEN PRACTICE! LET YOUR IMAGINATION GO.   G.F.H.

DON'T TRY TO COPY M-E-!

ZIP

OR ANYBODY

DEVELOP YOUR OWN STYLE ...

CERTAIN SHAPES ARE INTERESTING TO EXPLORE AS BASES FOR SPIRITED CREATURES. OBSERVE MR. OVAL PATE ON THE OPPOSITE PAGE. HIS TIE INCREASES IN LENGTH AS THE WHEELS ON HIS SKATES TURN FASTER.

UNFORTUNATELY, THE END OF MR. PATE'S CRAVAT BECOMES ENTANGLED IN A MISGUIDED SKATE AND --- **WHAM!**

THINK! THINK! THINK!

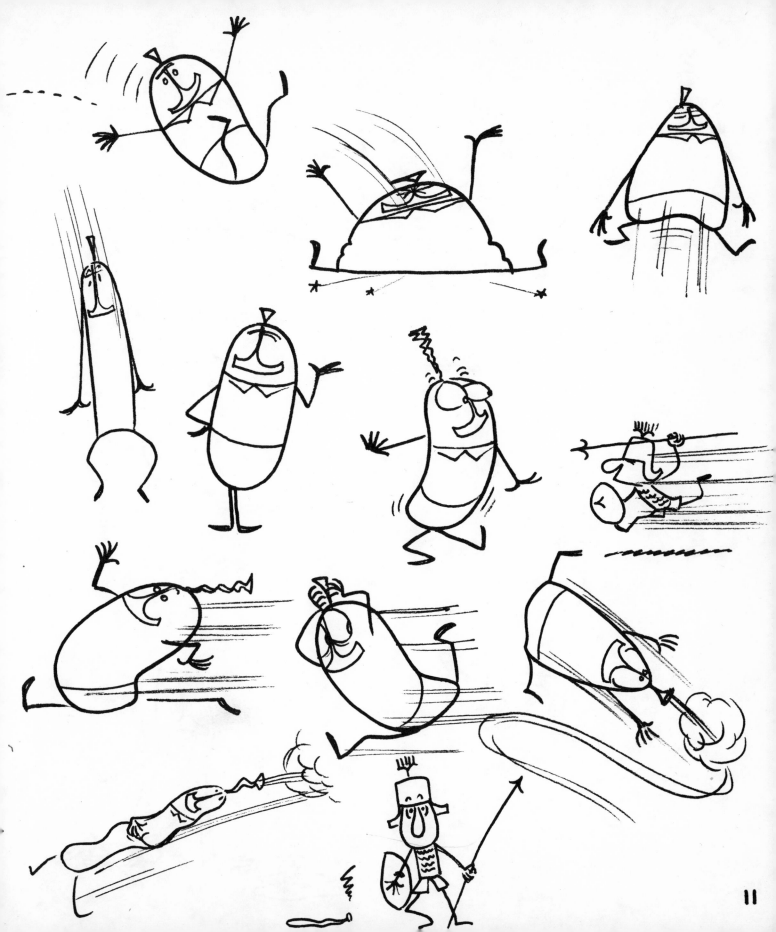

11

YOU WERE WRONG IN WHAT YOU WERE ABOUT TO SAY ANYHOW! LOOK AT YOUR HEAD! IT'S POINTED-- NOT EGG-SHAPED! (PARDON THE EXPRESSION)

--AND SOMETIMES YOU ARE MIGHTY SQUARE!

AND WHEN THEY
PUT THE SQUEEZE ON
YOU TO MEET A
DEADLINE---HA!

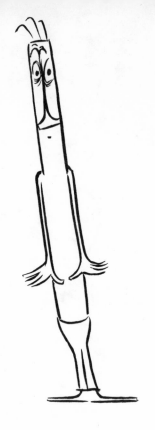

STOP "YOLKING" AROUND
AND TELL THEM THAT ALL
HEADS ARE NOT, ER, EGG-
SHAPED, BALLOON-HEAD.

THAT EGG
MADE ME
SO MAD
I COULD ·······

····· CRY

BUT I'LL
SMILE INSTEAD
BECAUSE HE
WAS RIGHT.

HA-HA-**HA** !

OH WELL !
IF YOU ARE
STILL WITH
ME LET'S
GO ON ----

JUST A MOMENT!

I'M A-O-K NOW! I CALL YOUR ATTENTION TO THE IMPORTANCE OF HANDS AND FEET IN GETTING COMPLETE FEELING INTO A CARTOON. OBSERVE THE EXPRESSIVENESS CREATED THROUGH THE HANDS AND FEET OF THE CHARACTERS ON THESE TWO PAGES.

19

21

DID YOU KNOW THAT YOU
DON'T HAVE ANY
EARS?

I READ LIPS! BUT EARS
CAN BE QUITE
USEFUL ---
AND EXPRESSIVE!

TALK ABOUT MY FAILINGS! I'VE SEEN MORE HAIR ON AN EGGPLANT!

I CAN COMB MY HAIR TO GET DIFFERENT EFFECTS--

I CAN ALSO CUT IT.

FROM THE WIG BOUTIQUE!

HAIR IS AFFECTED BY VARIOUS KINDS OF SITUATIONS.

--AND GLASSES

IT'S LIKE I WAS SAYING, MR. PROBOSCIS, IF MY FRIENDS WANT TO CARTOON, THEY MUST BE WELL-ACQUAINTED WITH FACIAL EXPRESSIONS ---
- VARIATIONS ON SHAPE OF HEADS, NOSES, EARS (MOST PEOPLE HAVE THEM), EYES, MOUTHS, HAIR, BEARDS.
- HOW DIFFERENT MOODS AND ACTIONS AFFECT FEATURES.
- HOW THE EYES, NOSE, MOUTH, EARS AND HAIR INTERACT IN EXPRESSING A FEELING.

HOW TO EXAGGERATE TO CREATE INTEREST.

WELL, I'M GOING TO STRAIGHTEN MY BONNET AND GET GOING. HERE COMES A GAL AND SHE LOOKS LIKE SHE HAS FIRE IN HER EYES!

I WOULD LIKE TO ADD A FEW MORE THINGS, **IF** YOU DON'T MIND.

WE GALS CAN MAKE CERTAIN--UH, CHANGES WITH MAKE-UP AND--ER--WELL YOU KNOW!

STUDY THE LATEST FASHION
MAGAZINES TO KEEP
UP ON LADIES WEARING
APPAREL. THEN USE
YOUR IMAGINATION.
EXAGGERATE!

MANY THANKS
FOR BEING SO
KIND TO LET ME
GET MY
TWO CENTS IN!

7.

8.

9.

DID YOU NOTICE HOW THE FACIAL FEATURES, ARMS, LEGS, AND ENTIRE BODY WERE COORDINATED TO GIVE FULL EXPRESSION IN EACH OF THOSE DELIGHTFUL SCENES?

WHILE I AM RECUPERATING I WILL TELL YOU ABOUT MY PAST PROWESS AS AN ATHLETE.

THEY CALLED ME "FIRE-BALL".

1.

2.

3.

4.

5.

6. UH -- THAT COULD HAPPEN TO ANY OF US.

UH --
TURN
THE
PAGE

KIDS!

HOW ABOUT GIVING US A BREAK!

39

HORSGUIN

GIRAFAROO

SNAKRICH

RAT-TLE

ALLIGABBIT

YOUR CARTOON MAY OCCUPY A SINGLE SPACE OR IT MAY BE A SEQUENCE, REQUIRING A SERIES OF SPACES. FIRST, DETERMINE THE SIZE OF THE SPACE(S). THEN ARRANGE THOSE ELEMENTS TO BE INCLUDED IN THE MOST INTERESTING WAY! USE JUST THAT MUCH THAT IS NECESSARY TO TELL THE STORY EFFECTIVELY.

LET ME ILLUSTRATE. I'LL JUST STEP IN HERE.

-- AND SIT DOWN.

HERE COMES AN EXCITED CHARACTER. WONDER WHAT HE WANTS.

GET THE POINT?

SIZE RELATIONSHIPS OF PEOPLE, CHILDREN, ANIMALS, OBJECTS, BUILDINGS, ARE IMPORTANT TO THE CARTOONIST. AIM FOR UNUSUAL ARRANGEMENTS... EXAGGERATE!

THAT'S MY BROTHER STANDING ON THE CORNER. THIS SAME BACKGROUND COULD BE USED FOR HIM OR ME. MY SIZE IN RELATION TO THE BUILDINGS INDICATES THAT I AM CLOSER TO YOU THAN HE IS. NOTE THE UNUSUAL PERSPECTIVE!

TO STRENGTHEN YOUR ABILITY TO DRAW OUTDOOR SCENES TAKE YOUR SKETCH BOOK WITH YOU AND PRACTICE DRAWING THE SCENE AROUND YOU.

44

I WOULD LIKE TO PAUSE HERE FOR A MOMENT TO TELL YOU HOW I DEVELOPED INTO THE CHARMING PERSONALITY THAT I AM. THERE WAS A TIME WHEN I WAS BUILT LIKE THE FELLOW ON THE EXTREME LEFT. THEN-- G-R-A-D-U-A-L-L-Y→

ME AND MY SHADOWS!

47

LETTERING FOR CARTOONS SHOULD BE SIMPLE AND EASY-TO-READ. GUIDE LINES SHOULD BE USED TO KEEP THE WORDS ON A STRAIGHT LINE. A WORD MAY BE **EMPHASIZED** BY MAKING IT LARGER, **BOLDER**, OR BY <u>UNDERLINING</u> IT. SOME WORDS MAY BE DRAWN TO REFLECT THE MEANING OF THE WORD.

STOP

SLOW

CRASH

BOING

49

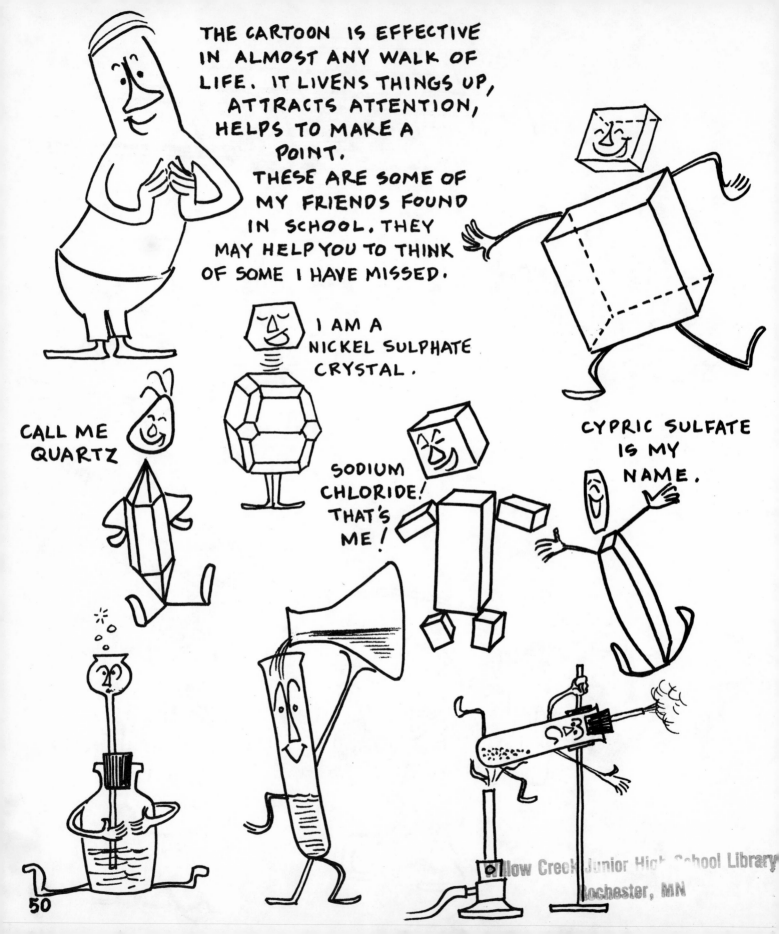

A POLYHEDRON WITH
FOUR FACES IS A
TETRAHEDRON

TWO TETRAHEDRONS
ARE SIMILAR IF---

IF A PLANE
INTERSECTS
A SPHERE--

NEGATIVE CHARGES ON A
SEALING WAX STICK NEUTRALIZE
POSITIVE CHARGES ON PITH BALL.

LIKE CHARGES REPEL.

DRY CELLS
IN A SERIES.

51

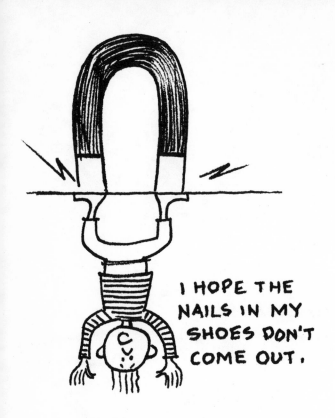

I HOPE THE NAILS IN MY SHOES DON'T COME OUT.

A GLOBE CAN HELP US LOCATE INTERESTING PLACES AND --

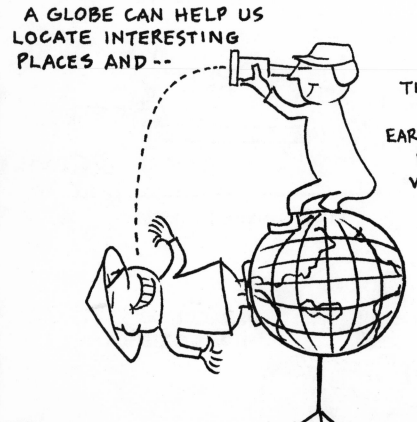

THREE-QUARTERS OF THE EARTH'S SURFACE IS COVERED WITH WATER!

BEING THRIFTY COUNTS UP!

KEEP FIRST AID SUPPLIES **HANDY**

FAMILIAR OBJECTS LEND THEMSELVES TO EXCITING ANIMATION. THESE SHOULD START YOU THINKING.

THE CARTOON CAN BE AN EFFECTIVE ATTENTION-GETTER IN MANY PARTS OF THE SCHOOL PROGRAM.

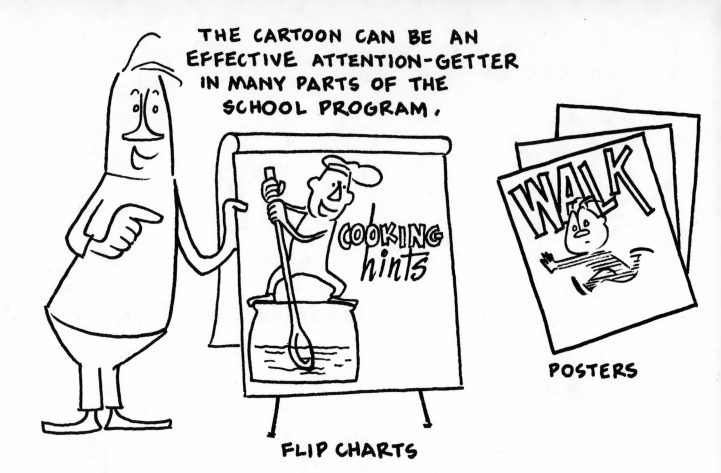

POSTERS

FLIP CHARTS

CHALKBOARDS

BULLETIN BOARDS

DISPLAY CASES

FLANNEL BOARDS

THE ELEMENT
OF SURPRISE IS A
MAJOR FACTOR
IN
CARTOONING.

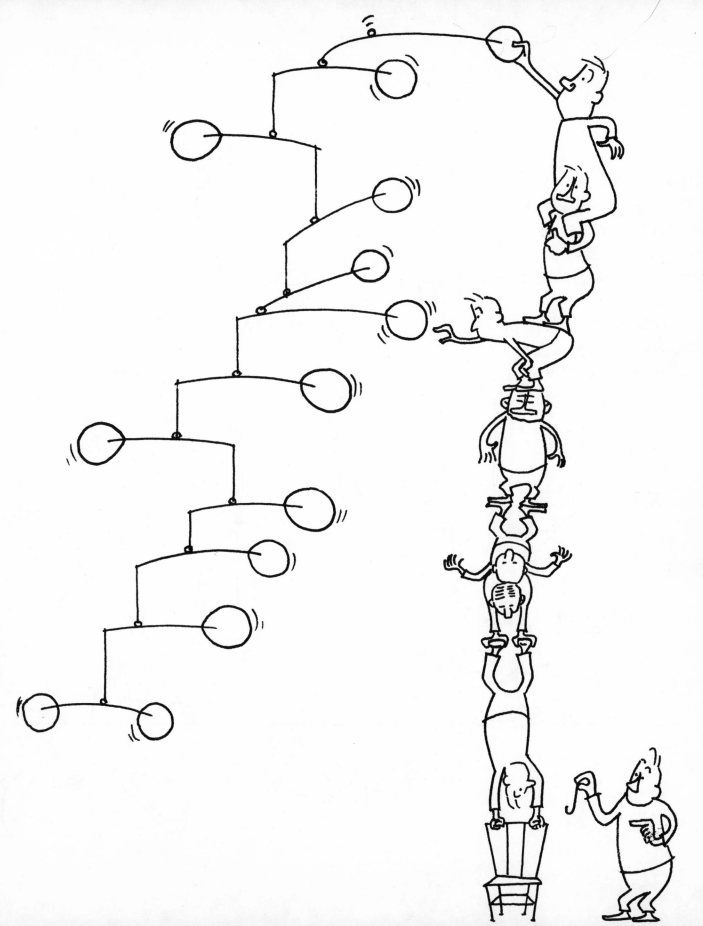

YOUR ABILITY
TO DRAW CARTOON
FIGURES WILL BE
ENHANCED BY
REGULAR SKETCHING
OF THE
COMMONPLACE
OCCURRENCES OF
DAY TO DAY LIVING.

THERE ARE MANY
DIFFERENT MATERIALS
AND TECHNIQUES
THAT MAY BE USED
TO ACHIEVE
VARIOUS EFFECTS.
HERE ARE SOME.

BRUSH AND INK

PEN AND INK

BRUSH & INK,
SHADING SCREENS

INK WASH

STRONG LIGHT TO CREATE INTERESTING SHADOWS

FELT PEN & SHADING SCREEN BACKGROUND

61

TECHNICALLY SPEAKING, THERE ARE TWO TYPES OF CARTOON DRAWINGS. ONE IS A LINE DRAWING; THE OTHER, A HALFTONE. WHILE THE SAME SUBJECT MAY BE PRESENTED IN EITHER TECHNIQUE, THE ESSENTIAL DIFFERENCE IS ONE OF TONAL EFFECTS.

ORDINARILY, LINE DRAWINGS ARE RENDERED WITH SUCH MATERIALS AS PEN AND INK, BRUSH AND INK, CRAYON, FELT PEN. SHADING IS ACHIEVED THROUGH THE USE OF LINES DRAWN IN VARIOUS COMBINATIONS. FOR EXAMPLE, WHEN USING PEN AND INK A TONE OF GRAY MAY BE REPRESENTED BY CROSS-HATCHING THE PEN STROKES. THE CLOSER THE STROKES, THE DARKER THE TONE.

COMMERCIALLY PREPARED SHADING
SCREENS MAY BE USED ALSO TO GET
VARIOUS OTHER LINE DRAWING FEAT-
URES. THESE SCREENS, AVAILABLE
IN NUMEROUS PATTERNS COMPOSED
OF DOTS, LINES, OR SPECIFIC DESIGNS,
MAY BE OBTAINED THROUGH LOCAL
ART DEALERS. SHADING SCREEN
PATTERNS ARE ON CLEAR ACETATE,
BACKED UP WITH A THIN COAT OF
WAX WHICH ACTS AS AN ADHESIVE.
THE SCREENS ARE USED BY PLACING
THE DESIRED PATTERN OVER THE
DRAWING AND CUTTING IT TO FIT.
SHADING SCREENS ARE USED ONLY
IN COMBINATION WITH LINE DRAW-
INGS.

WASH DRAWINGS (HALFTONES),
CHARACTERIZED BY THEIR GRADED
TONES, ARE ACCOMPLISHED
WITH SUCH MATERIALS AS INK
AND CLEAR WATER (INK WASH),
BLACK WATER COLOR AND CLEAR
WATER, LAMP BLACK AND
CLEAR WATER. TONES MAY BE
FLAT OR VARIED, ACCORDING
TO THE DESIRES OF THE ARTIST,
LIGHT TINTS ARE MADE BY
ADDING CLEAR WATER TO THE
MEDIUM; DEEPER SHADES, BY
ADDING MORE PIGMENT TO
THE WATER,

CUT OUT CARTOON FIGURES
ARE VERY EFFECTIVE IN THE
PROMOTION OF SCHOOL
ACTIVITIES. IF YOU HAVE A
CUT-AWL*, WALLBOARD MAY
BE USED FOR THIS PURPOSE.
POSTER BOARD CARTOONS
MAY BE CUT OUT WITH
A SHARP STENCIL
KNIFE. THESE CARTOON
FIGURES WILL STAND
ALONE WHEN BACKED UP
WITH AN EASEL.

WOOD STRIPS SHOULD BE USED
TO SUPPORT A CARTOON FIGURE
CUT OUT OF WALLBOARD.

* THE CUT-AWL IS AN ELECTRICALLY POWERED
TOOL USED IN CUTTING LETTERS, FIGURES
AND SHAPES FROM SUCH MATERIALS AS
PRESSED WOOD, PLYWOOD, WALLBOARD,
PLASTICS, METAL. THE BLADE IS ATTACHED
TO ALLOW FOR THE CUTTING OF COMPLETE
CIRCLES AND INTRICATE CURVES IN A
SINGLE OPERATION.

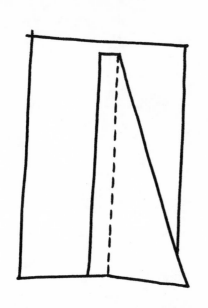

A SIMPLE CARDBOARD EASEL, SCORED
TO FOLD OUT, MAY BE GLUED TO THE BACK OF
A POSTER BOARD FIGURE.

CUT OUT CARTOONS MAY BE DISPLAYED ALSO
FROM AN ORDINARY EASEL OR THEY MAY BE
SUSPENDED WITH A LENGTH OF STRING OR WIRE.

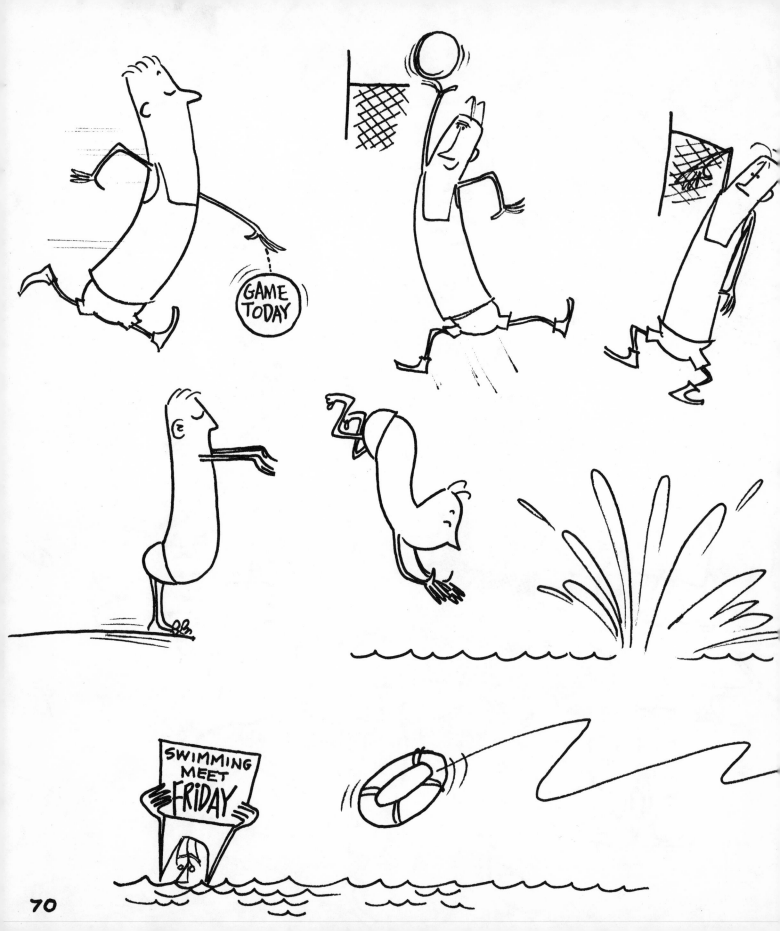

71